MY PET
Kitten

Honor Head

Photographs by Jane Burton

RAINTREE
STECK-VAUGHN
PUBLISHERS

A Harcourt Company

Austin   New York
www.steck-vaughn.com

Published by Raintree Steck-Vaughn Publishers, an imprint of Steck-Vaughn Company.

Editors: Claire Edwards, Erik Greb
Art Director: Max Brinkmann
Designer: Rosamund Saunders
Illustrator: Pauline Bayne

Printed in Singapore

1 2 3 4 5 6 7 8 9 0 LB 03 02 01 00

Library of Congress Cataloging-in-Publication Data

Head, Honor.
   Kitten/Honor Head; photographs by Jane Burton.
   p. cm.—(My pet)
   Summary: Describes the physical characteristics and habits of kittens and tells how to care for them as pets.
   ISBN 0-7398-2884-3 (hardcover)
   ISBN 0-7398-3011-2 (softcover)
   1. Kittens—Juvenile literature. [1. Cats. 2. Animals—Infancy. 3. Pets.] I. Burton, Jane, ill. II. Title.

SF445.7 .H43 2000
636.8'07—dc21
                    00–027052

Contents

My Kitten

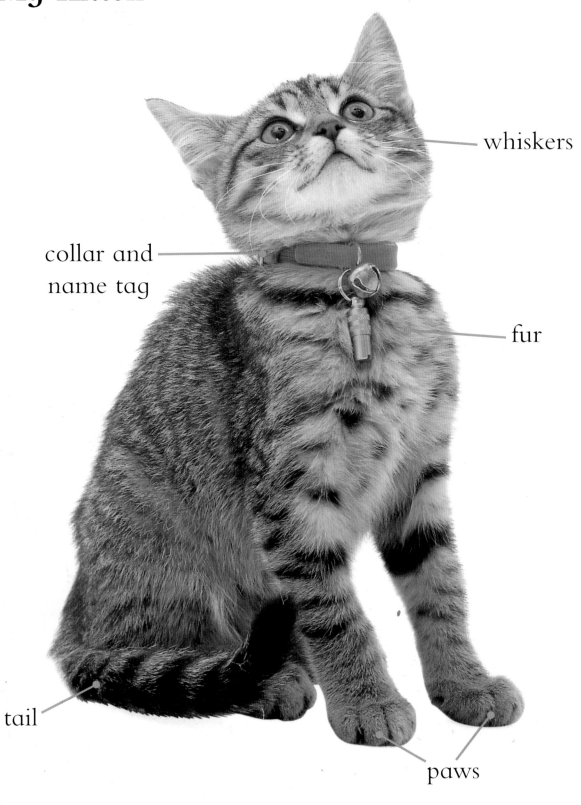

whiskers

collar and
name tag

fur

tail

paws

4

It's fun to have your own pet.

Kittens look very sweet and are fun to play with, but they need to be looked after carefully.

A kitten needs to be fed every day and brushed regularly. It will also have to be trained. Most of all, remember that your kitten will grow into a cat and be with you for a long time.

Young children with pets should always work with an adult. For further notes, please see page 32.

5

There are many different types of cats.

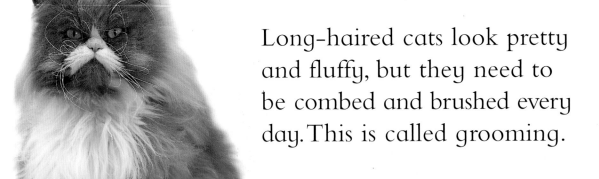

Long-haired cats look pretty and fluffy, but they need to be combed and brushed every day. This is called grooming.

Short-haired cats do not need to be groomed as often.

Cats have many different colors and markings.

This is a tortoiseshell cat.

This is a ginger cat.

This is a tabby cat.

There are many different kinds of cats. Siamese cats have short, sleek fur, and a long, pointed face. Maine Coon cats are bigger and very fluffy.

A pregnant cat needs somewhere safe to have her kittens.

A pregnant cat will look for a quiet and safe place to have her kittens. An old blanket or some torn-up newspaper will make her feel more comfortable.

When a cat becomes pregnant, her shape changes. Her stomach gets bigger and rounder.

8

When she is very pregnant, a mother cat doesn't move around much. She may be stroked gently but not picked up.

When a mother cat is ready to have her kittens, she stops eating. Soon she will have her first kitten. It will take a long time for all the kittens to be born.

9

When kittens are born, they cannot see, hear, or walk.

A newborn kitten
is a terrible mess!
Soon its mother
licks it clean.

Kittens find their way to their mother's milk by smell. Drinking their mother's milk is called suckling. Kittens first start to purr when they are suckling.

When they have finished feeding, the kittens fall asleep in a heap. The mother cat goes off to eat and rest. The kittens look sweet, but they are too young to be touched.

If a kitten feels lost or frightened, it will meow loudly for its mother.

Kittens grow very quickly.

The mother cat moves her kittens by picking them up in her mouth. People should never pick up a kitten or a cat by the neck.

When a kitten is one week old, it cannot walk yet. It crawls along the floor.

The mother cat keeps her kittens clean by licking them. This also teaches the kittens how to lick themselves clean.

After three weeks, the kitten is learning to walk. It is very wobbly on its legs and keeps falling over.

When the kitten is eight weeks old, it is old enough to leave its mother.

Now the kitten is six weeks old. It can run and jump and begin to explore its home.

Kittens are very playful.

As the kittens grow older, they begin to play together. They pretend to fight, but they don't hurt each other.

The mother cat teaches her kittens how to hunt by playing with a toy mouse.

If a kitten is healthy and happy, it will always find something to play with.

Kittens will love playing with you as long as you are gentle. Play with a special cat toy or a piece of string or ball of paper.

Make sure your kitten's toys are safe. They should have no metal or sharp parts.

15

You have to take care of your kitten.

Your kitten must be trained to use a litter box. Put the litter box in a quiet, private place.

Kittens need small meals four times a day. Always keep the bowls clean. Rinse them well after you have washed them.

By eight weeks, kittens can eat solid food. Leave your pet alone when it is eating. Always give your kitten clean, fresh water to drink.

Make sure your pet has a quiet, warm place to sleep. Put a soft pillow or a blanket in a basket or box.

Be gentle with your kitten.

When you want your kitten to come to you, hold out your hand. Let it sniff you. Then, pick it up gently. If the kitten doesn't want to be picked up, leave it alone.

Always stroke your kitten gently from the head down the back toward its tail. Your kitten will also like to have its head and ears rubbed and its chin tickled.

When you pick up your kitten, hold it under its bottom with one hand. Then, gently support its body with the other hand. Do not squeeze it around the middle with its legs dangling.

Never grab your kitten or pull its tail. Your kitten is small, and you might hurt it.

Kittens like to keep clean.

A kitten spends a lot of time cleaning itself. It uses its paws to wash its face. It licks its fur to keep it smooth.

Comb and brush your kitten from the head towards the tail. Comb it gently, then brush it. If it has any knots you can't untangle, take it to the vet. Never pull its fur.

Most kittens enjoy being brushed if you are gentle. Use a special brush and comb.

When a long-haired kitten licks itself, it swallows loose hairs. The hairs can form a hairball in a kitten's stomach and make it sick. If this happens, take your kitten to the vet.

If you groom your pet carefully, it should not get hairballs.

If your kitten keeps scratching, it may have fleas. Ask your vet for help.

Kittens enjoy exploring and getting into mischief.

Kittens will explore their home from top to bottom. They climb on furniture and crawl under tables. Give your pet a box to explore.

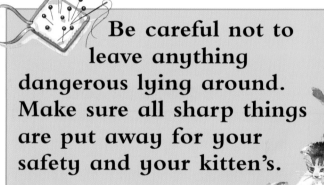

Be careful not to leave anything dangerous lying around. Make sure all sharp things are put away for your safety and your kitten's.

If your kitten scratches the furniture, say "No" in a firm voice. Buy it a scratching post from a pet store. Never shout at or hit your kitten.

Make sure your kitten does
not eat indoor
flowers or plants.
They may be
poisonous.

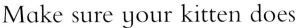

Before your kitten
explores outside, it will
need a collar with your
address or telephone
number on it. Make
sure the collar is not too
tight. Don't allow your
kitten out until it has had
all its shots.

Your kitten will need to visit the vet.

A kitten should be taken to the vet for a checkup when it is about four weeks old. At 12 weeks it will need shots to keep it from catching any diseases. It will need another shot every year.

All kittens should be neutered when they are about five months old. This is to keep them from having unwanted kittens.

If your kitten stops eating, keeps sneezing, has runny eyes or dry fur, it might be sick. Put it in a special carrier and take it to the vet right away.

Cardboard carriers can be used for kittens and small cats. Bigger cats need stronger carriers.

How is your kitten feeling?

Your kitten will soon know your voice and smell. It may rub against you to say hello. If it holds its tail up in the air, it is pleased to see you.

If your kitten is angry or frightened, it will make itself look bigger by arching its back and fluffing up its fur. Do not touch your kitten if it does this.

When your kitten licks your hand, it is being friendly. If it kneads your lap or purrs, it is happy.

When your kitten is hungry, it will meow. Some kittens raise a paw to beg. Older kittens may beg by standing on their back legs.

If your kitten feels safe, it may lie on its back. Do not tickle its tummy. Most kittens do not like having their tummy touched.

Your kitten will soon grow up.

When your kitten is about a year old, you will see how grown up it looks. It will still enjoy playing, but be careful— it will have sharp teeth and claws.

As your cat grows older, it will be less playful, and will sleep more. But it will still like being stroked and talked to.

Cats can live for 20 years or more. But, like people, they grow old and die. If your pet is very ill or badly injured, it may also die.

You may feel sad when your pet dies, but you will be able to look back and remember all the happy times you had together.

Words to Remember

fleas Tiny biting insects that live in a cat's fur.

groom To brush and comb a cat.

knead What a cat does when it pushes its claws in and out against something.

litter box A cat's toilet.

mew The crying noise a very young kitten makes.

meow The crying noise a cat makes.

paws Cats' feet.

purr The noise a cat makes in its throat.

suckling When a kitten drinks its mother's milk, it is suckling.

vet An animal doctor.

whiskers The long hairs on a cat's face.

A newborn kitten cannot see or hear.

At eight weeks, a kitten is old enough to leave its mother.

At three weeks, a kitten is learning to walk.

At four weeks, a kitten grows its first teeth.

Index

Notes for Parents

A cat will give you and your family a great deal of pleasure, but it is a big responsibility. If you decide to buy a kitten for your child, you will need to ensure that the animal is healthy, happy, and safe. You will have to train and feed your pet, and care for it if it is sick. You will also have to work with your child with the animal until he or she is at least five years old. It will be your responsibility to make sure your child does not harm the kitten and learns to handle it correctly.

Here are some other points to think about before you decide to own a cat:

🐾 Is your home suitable for a cat? Do you have a yard, or will you have to keep a litter box in the house all the time? Are you near a main road? If you have a balcony, do not let your cat out on to it.

🐾 Do you have other pets? Will the kitten get along with them?

🐾 Who will look after your cat when you go on vacation?

Can you afford a kennel?

🐾 Kittens and cats need annual injections. Can you afford them?

🐾 If there is no one at home all day, it is better to have two cats together.

🐾 All cats should be neutered. Make sure you can afford the vet's fees.

🐾 Cats often bring dead or live animals, such as birds and mice, into the house.

🐾 Cats can live for 20 years or more, and may need expensive treatment as they grow older.

🐾 Cats can be microchipped to identify their owners. This may be safer and more reliable than wearing a collar.

This book is intended as an introduction only for young readers. If you have any questions about how to look after your kitten, you can contact the Humane Society of the U.S., 2100 L Street NW, Washington, DC 20037.